CHRISTMAS
COLOR BY NUMBER

THIS BOOK BELONGS TO

COLOR TEST PAGE

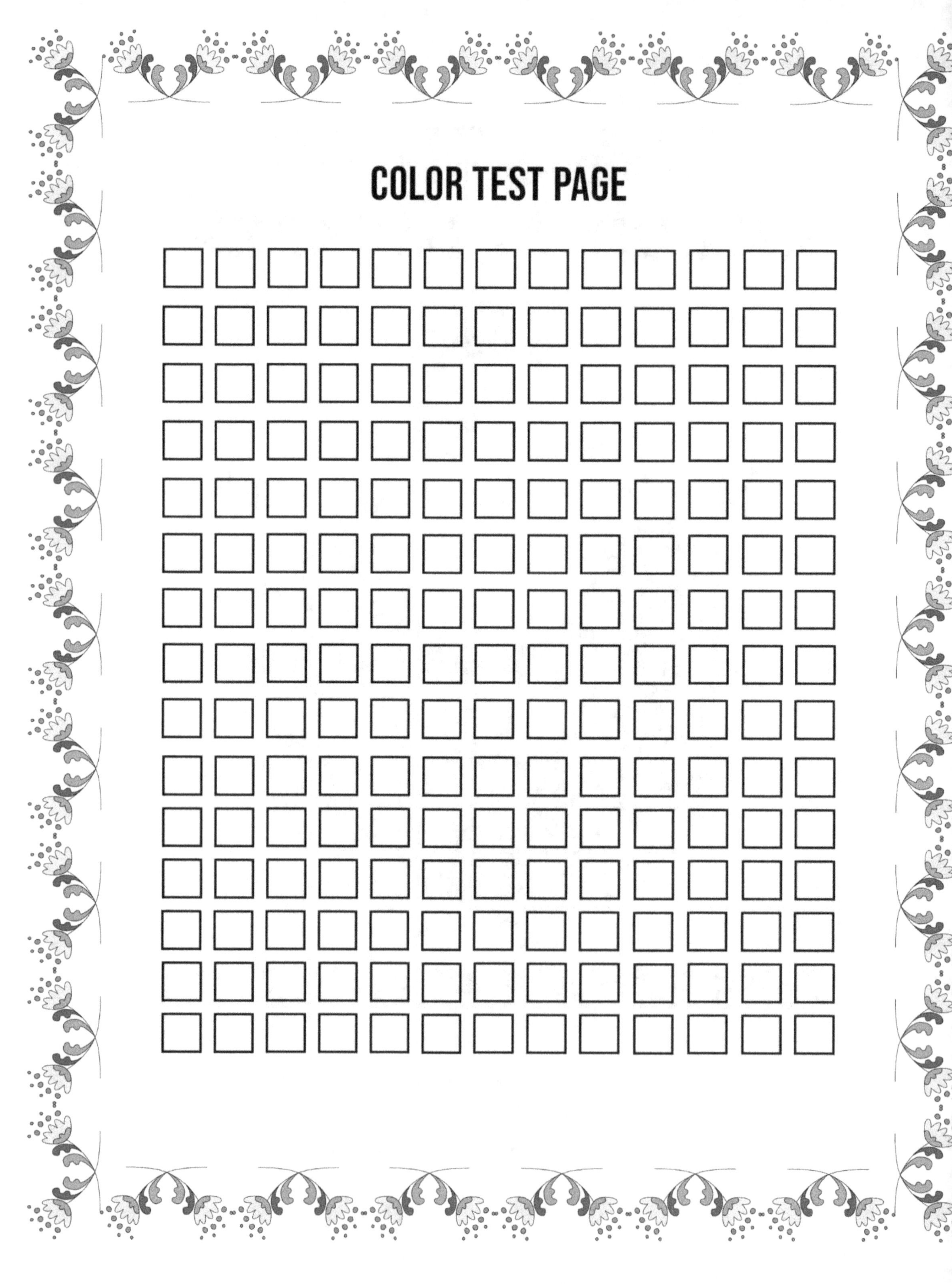

COLOR TEST PAGE

1.Red   2.Green   3.Narvik   4.Apache

5.Maroon   6.White   7.Black   8.Lime

1.Apache   2.Green   3.White   4.Red

5.Luxor Gold   5.Midnight Blue

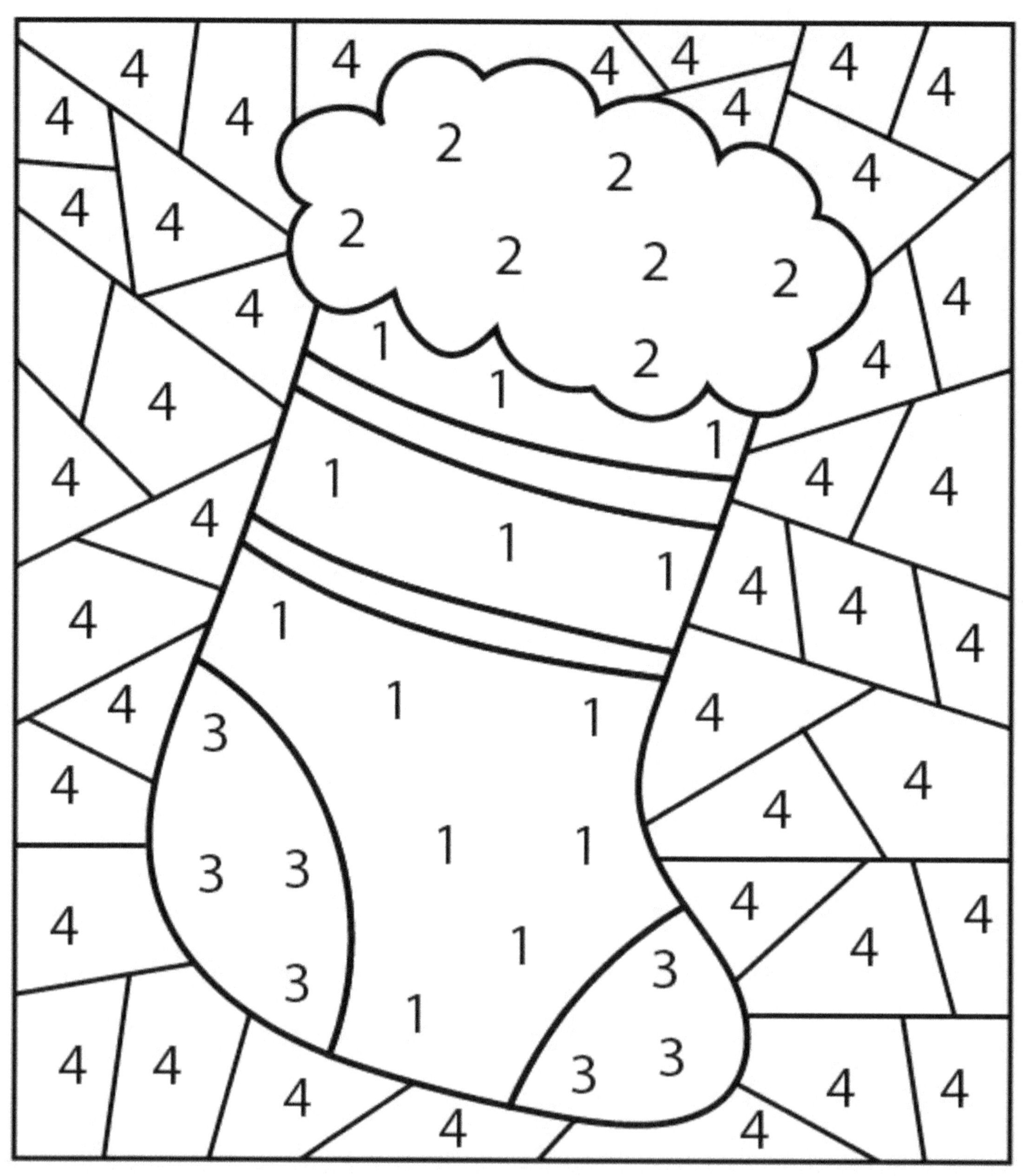

1.Scarlet   2.Ivory   3.Observatory

4.Aquamarine

1.Green   2.Red   3.Apache   4.Apache

5.Luxor Gold   6.Aqua

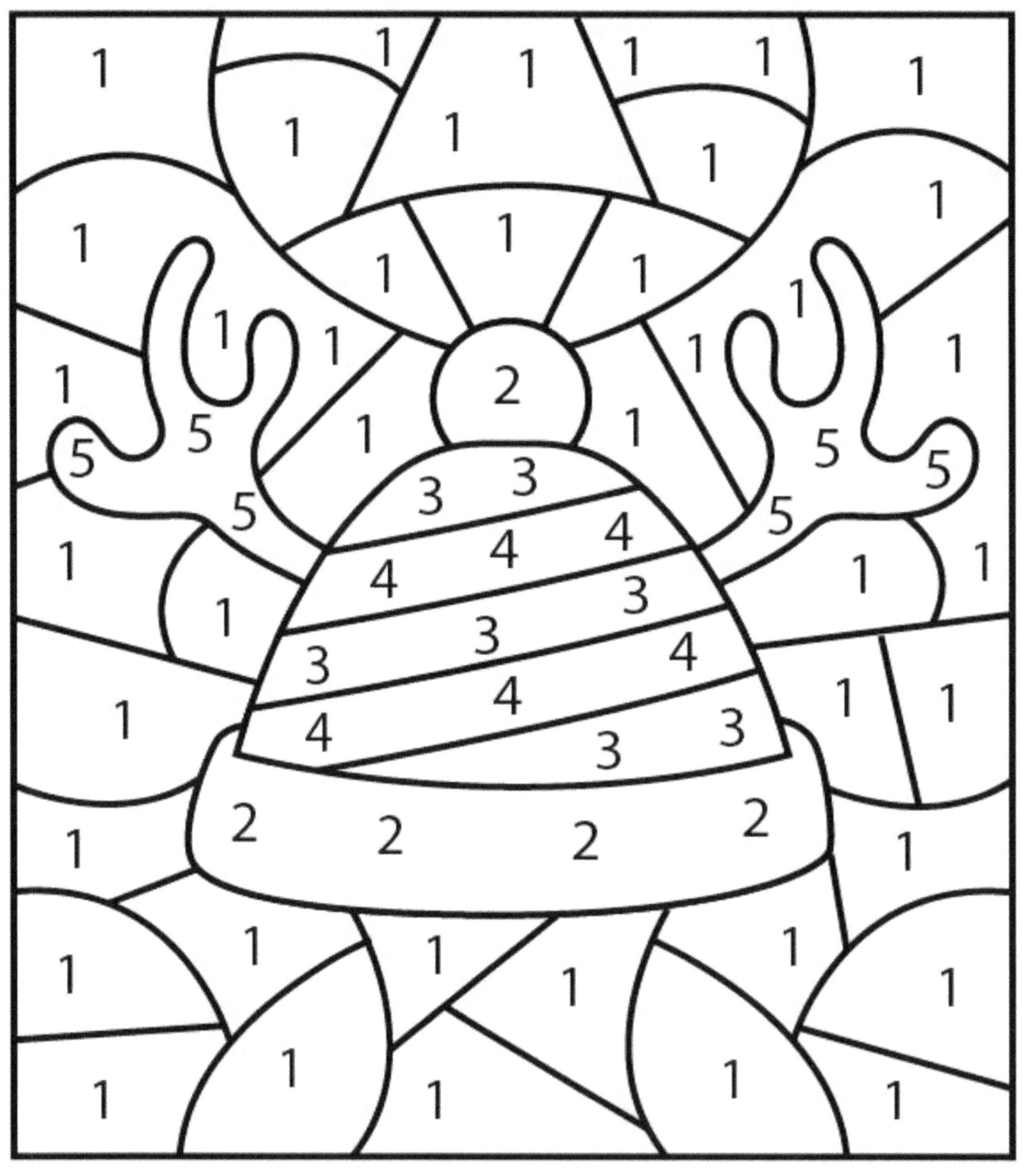

1.Aquamarine   2.White   3.Pigment Green

4.Cinnabar   5.Dark Goldenrod

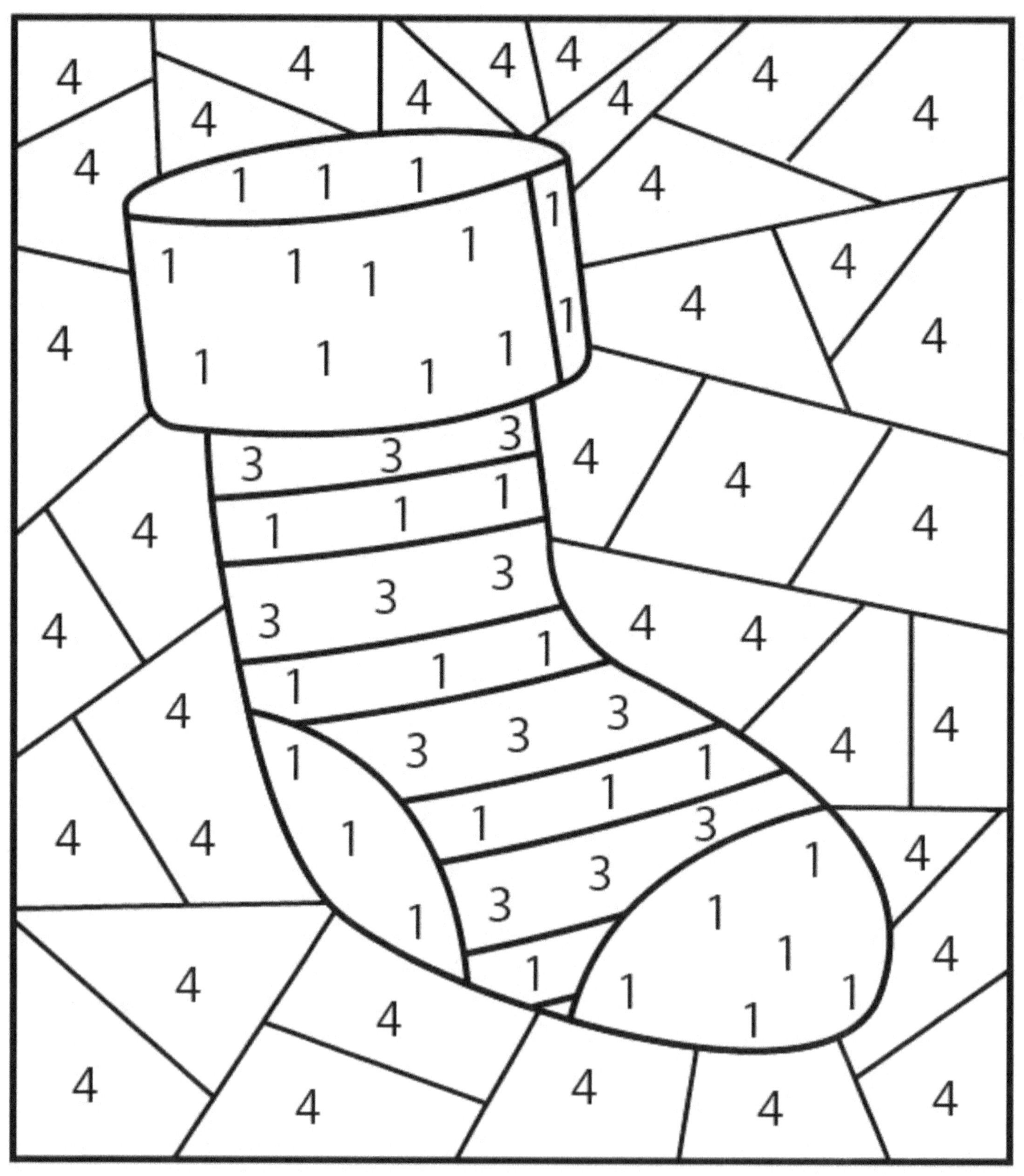

1.Deep Sky Blue   2.White   3.Cinnabar

4.Screamin' Green

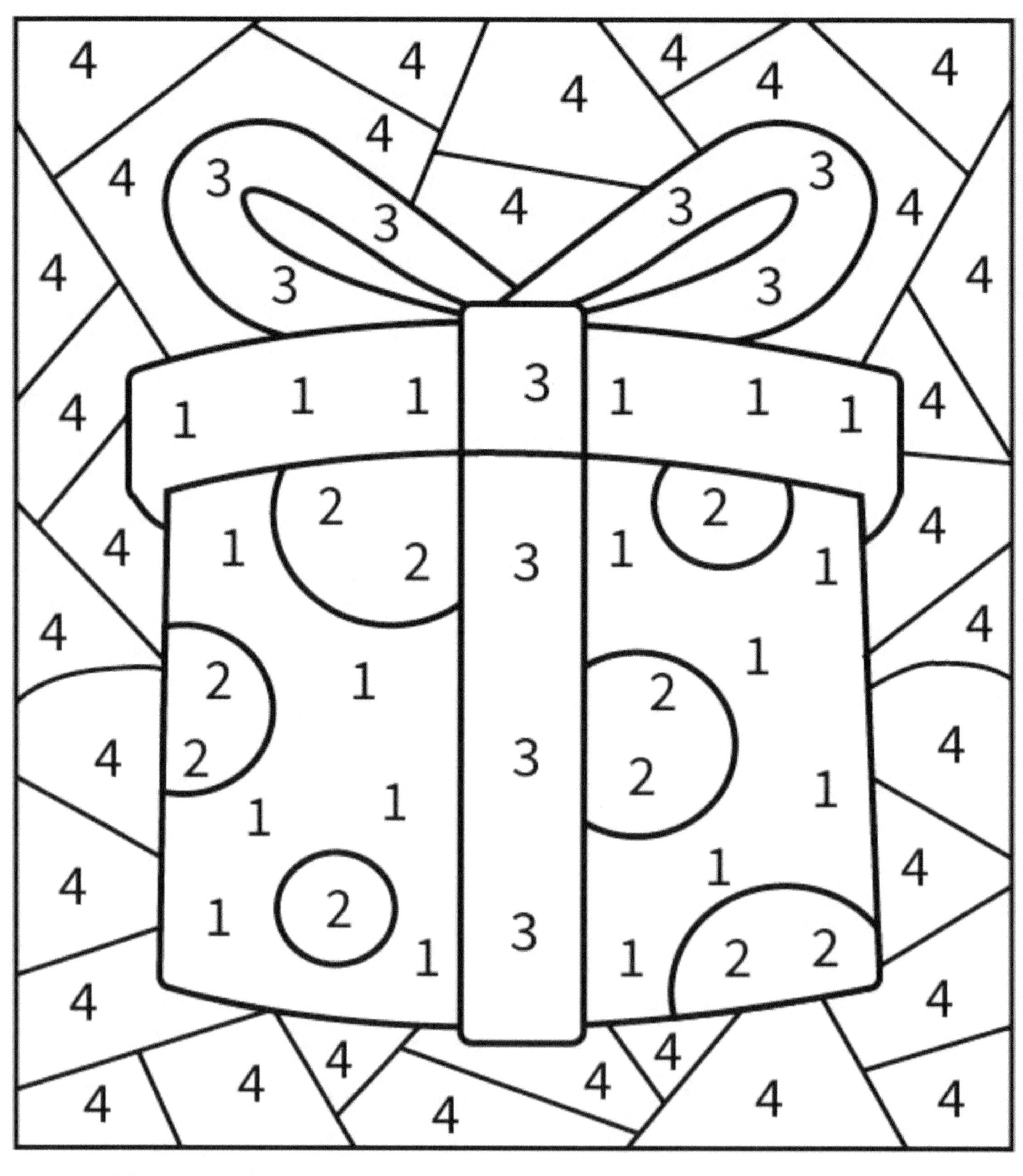

1.Cinnabar 2.White 3.Turbo

4.Aqua

1.Lightning Yellow   2.Deep Sky Blue   3.Turbo

4.White   5.Cinnabar   6.Pigment Green

1.Green   2.Red   3.Grenadier   4.Yellow

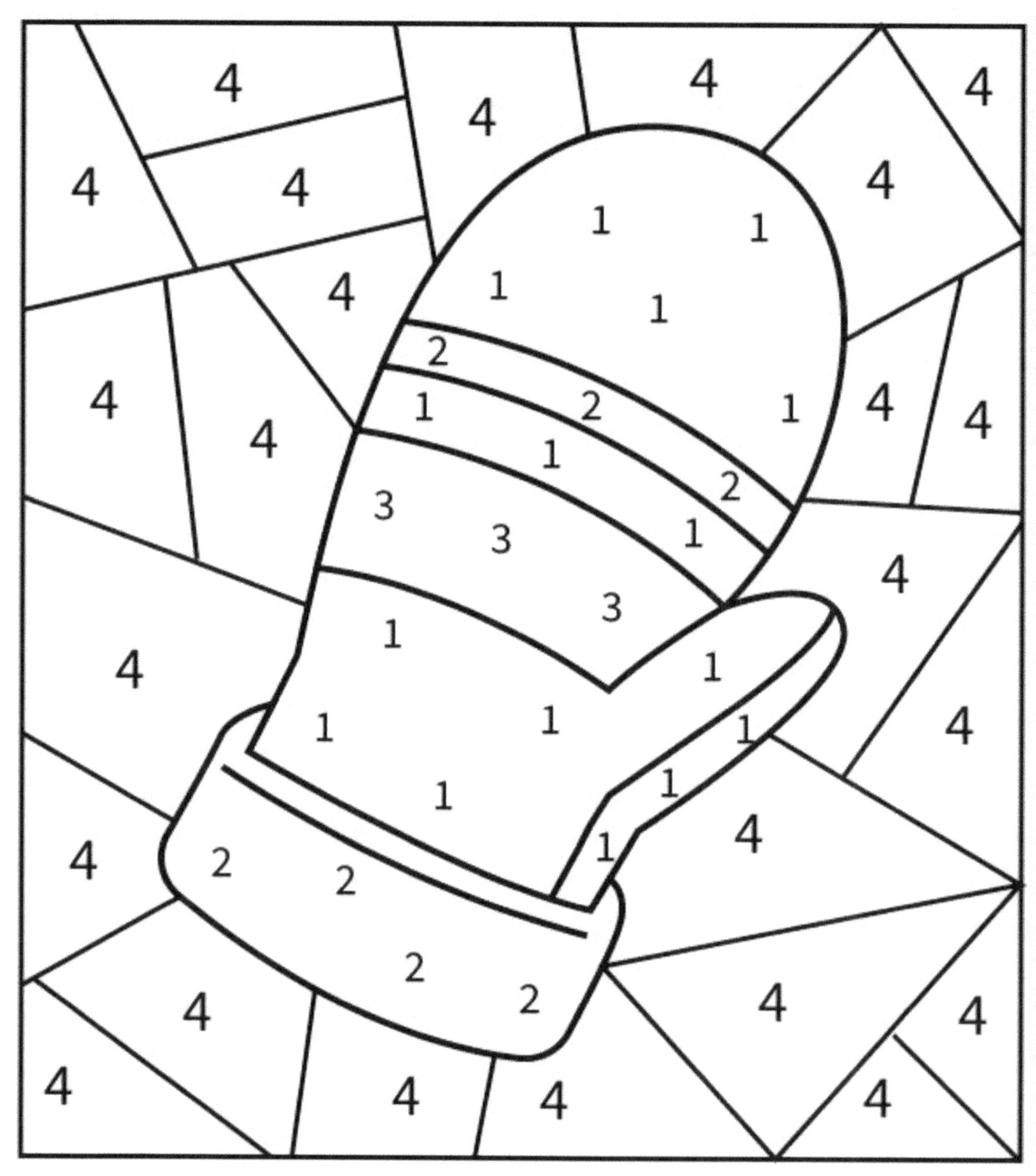

1.Pigment Green   2.Cinnabar   3.White

4.Aqua

0-No Color,1-Red,2-Green,3-Prussian Blue,4-Yellow,5-Flesh,6-Dark Green,7-Burnt Sienna

0-No Color,1-Red,2-Green,3-Burnt Sienna,4-Sky Blue,5-Flesh,6-Yellow Ochre

0-No Color,1-Red,2-Green,3-Burnt Sienna,4-Prussian Blue,5-Flesh,6-Yellow,7-Grey

0-No Color,1-Red,2-Green,3-Yellow,4-Prussian Blue,5-Burnt Sienna,6-Flesh,7-Grey

0-No color,1-Red,2-Green,3-Burnt Sienna,4-Yellow,5-Grey,6-Prussian Blue,7-Flesh

0-No Color,1-Green,2-Red,3-Burnt Sienna,4-Sky Blue,5-Yellow,6-Black,7-Flesh

0-No Color,1-Prussian Blue,2-Yellow,3-Burnt Sienna,4-Red,5-Yellow Ochre,6-Green,7-Flesh

0-No Color,1-Red,2-Yellow,3-Burnt Sienna,4-Brown,5-Orange,6-Flesh,7-Green,8-Sky Blue

0-No Color,1-Violet,2-Cream Yellow,4-Brown,5-Burnt Sienna,6-Green,7-Sky Blue,8-Yellow

1-Red,2-Yellow,3-Sky Blue,4-dark blue,5-Violet,6-Burnt Sienna,7-Flesh,8-Green

0-No Color,1-Red,2-Green,3-Yellow,4-Blue,5-Yellow Ochre,6-Flesh,7-Burnt Sienna

o-No color,1-Red,2-Sky Blue,3-Orange,4-violet,5-yellow Ochre,6-Burnt Sienna,7-Green

0-No color,1-Red,2-Yellow,3-Grey,4-Dark Blue,5-Green,6-Burnt Sienna

0-no color,1-red,2-burnt Sienna,3-grey,4-sky Blue,5-yellow,6-Flesh

0-No Color,1-Red,2-Yellow,3-Light blue,4-Green,5-Flesh,6-Orange,7-Burnt Sienna,8-Black

no color-0 ,Flesh-1 , Olive Green-2 , 3-Burnt Orange ,4-Blue , 5-Red, 6-Sky Blue

no color-0, Sky Blue-1, Orange-2, Burnt Sienna-3, Light Green-4, dark Green-5, Yellow Ochre-6

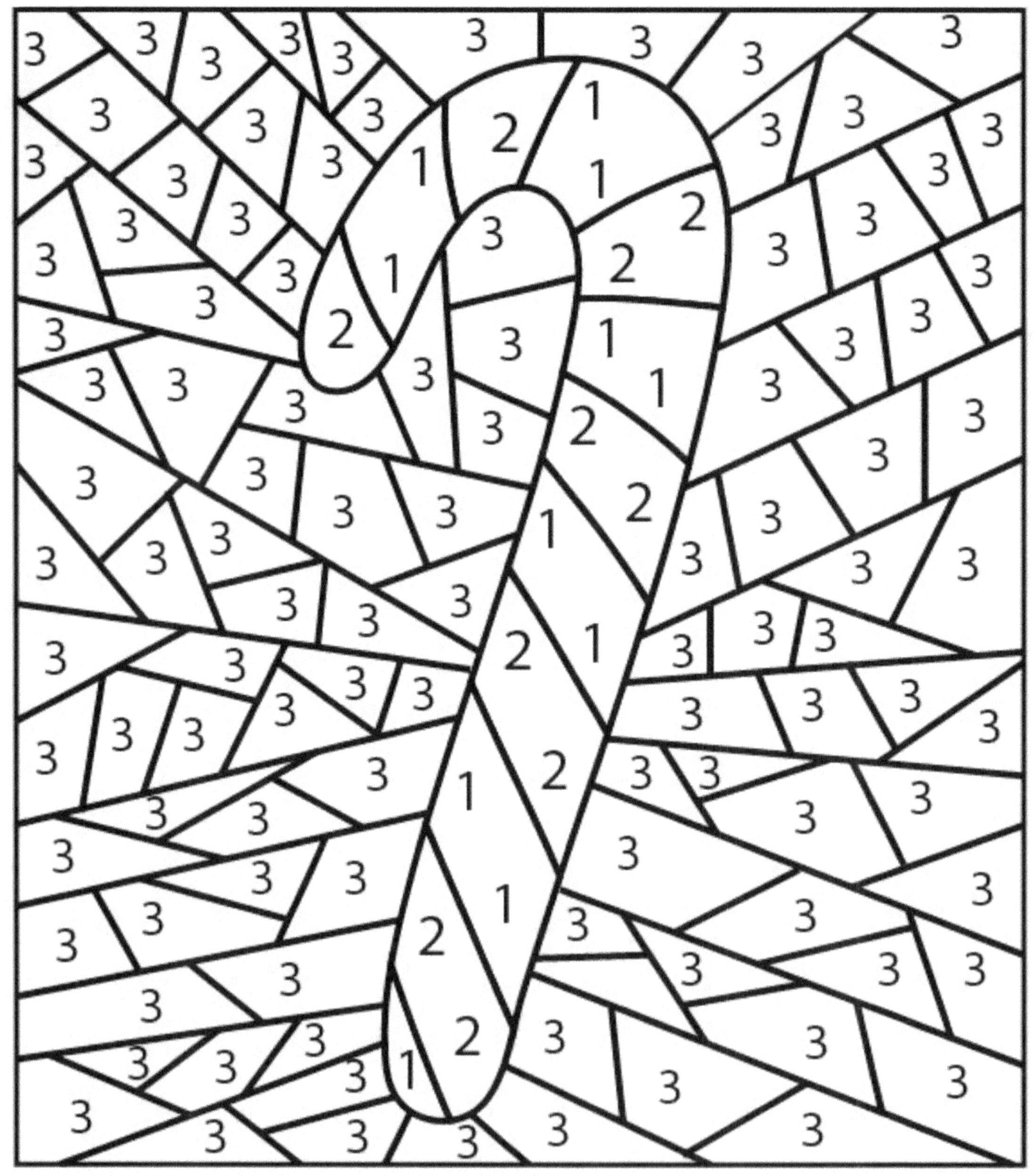

1.Red   2.White   3.Aqua

1.Red   2.Apache   3.Green   4.White
5.Aqua

1.Caper 2.Sandy Beach 3.Milano Red 4.Peru Tan

5. Summer Sky

1. Green
2. Dark Goldenrod
3. Red
4. Yellow
5. Deep Sky Blue
6. Ruby

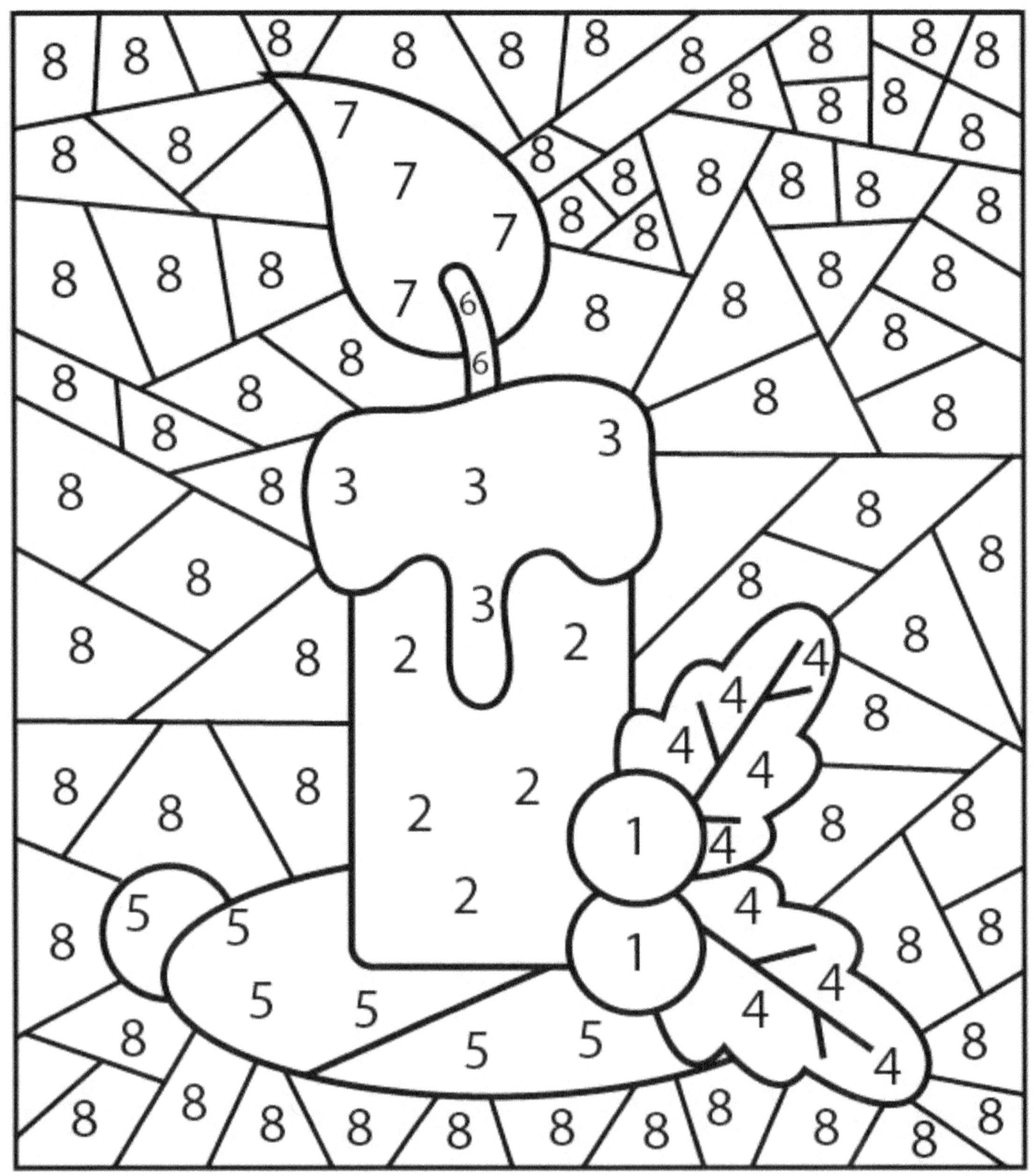

1.Red   2.Spray   3.White   4.Green

5.Prussian Blue   6.Black   7.Coral   8.Yellow

1.Red   2.Yellow Orange   3.Green   4.Aqua

1.Red   2.Green   3.Mandys Pink   4.Caper

5. Vivid Violet

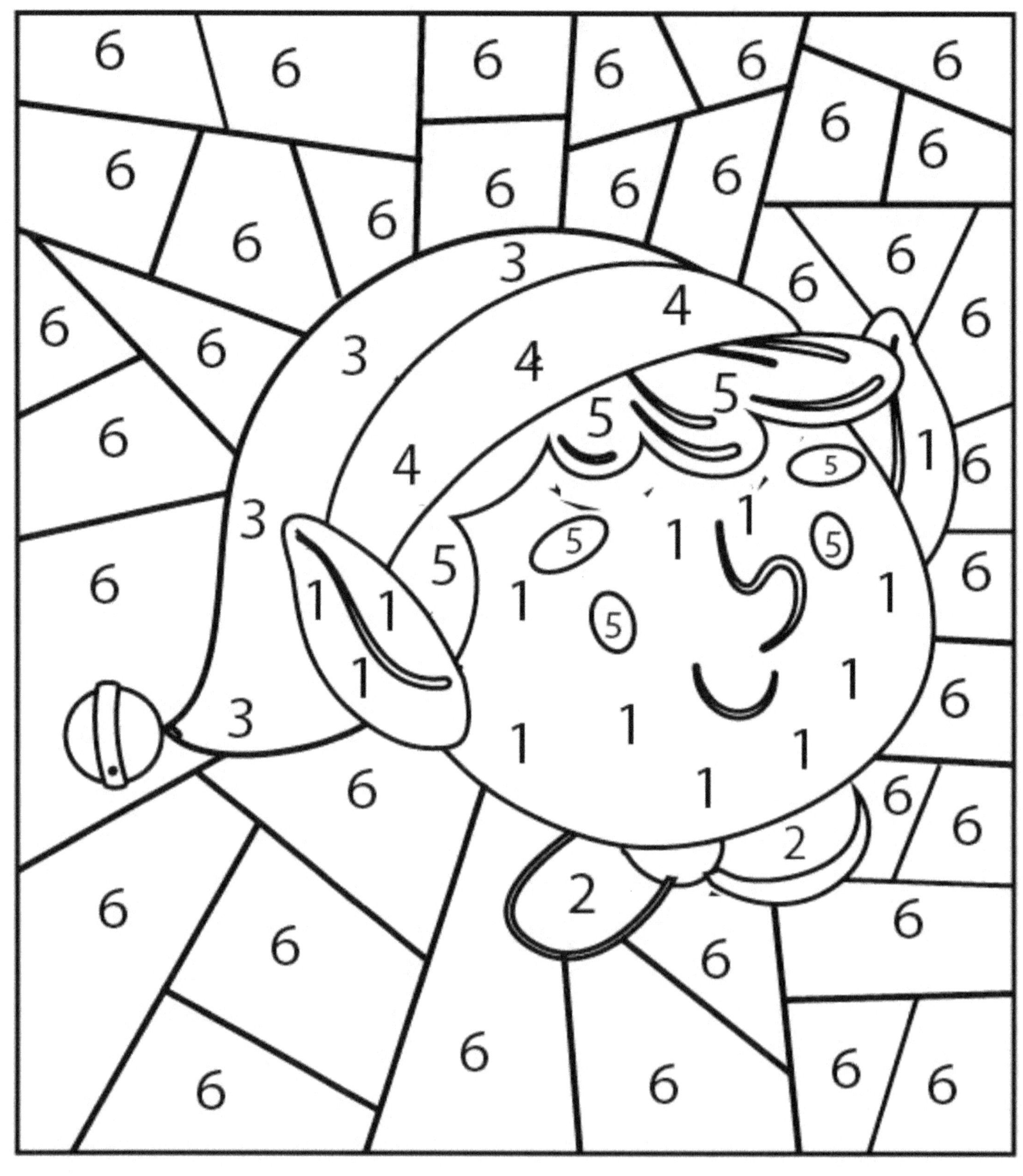

1.Romantic   2.Red   3.Green   4.White

5.Black   6.Yellow

1.Sandy Beach   2.Alert Tan   3.Zest   4.Green

5. Red   6. Dark Blue

1.Caper   2.Red   3.Milano Red   4.Grey Suit

5. Summer Sky

1	PURPLE		**2**	VIOLET
3	YELLOW		**4**	RED
5	PINK		**6**	ORANGE
7	SKY BLUE		**8**	GREEN
9	MEDIUM BROWN			

(1)	RED		(2)	WHITE
(3)	LIGHT BLUE		(4)	LIGHT BROWN
(5)	YELLOW		(6)	LIGHT PURPLE

(1)	LIGHT BROWN		(2)	DARK BROWN
(3)	WHITE		(4)	YELLOW
(5)	LIGHT BLUE		(6)	MEDIUM BLUE
(7)	LIGHT VIOLET		(8)	LIGHT GREEN
(9)	LIGHT ORANGE		(10)	PINK
(11)	MEDIUM ORANGE		(12)	RED
(13)	DARK GREEN		(14)	MEDIUM GREEN

(1)	**MEDIUM PINK**		(2)	**DARK PINK**
(3)	**RED**		(4)	**MEDIUM YELLOW**
(5)	**DARK YELLOW**		(6)	**LIGHT YELLOW**
(7)	**GREEN**		(8)	**MEDIUM BLUE**
(9)	**LIGHT BLUE**			

(1)	**DARK RED**	(2)	**DARK GREEN**
(3)	**LIGHT GREEN**	(4)	**LIGHT RED**
(5)	**LIGHT BROWN**	(6)	**MEDIUM BROWN**
(7)	**LIGHT BLUE**		

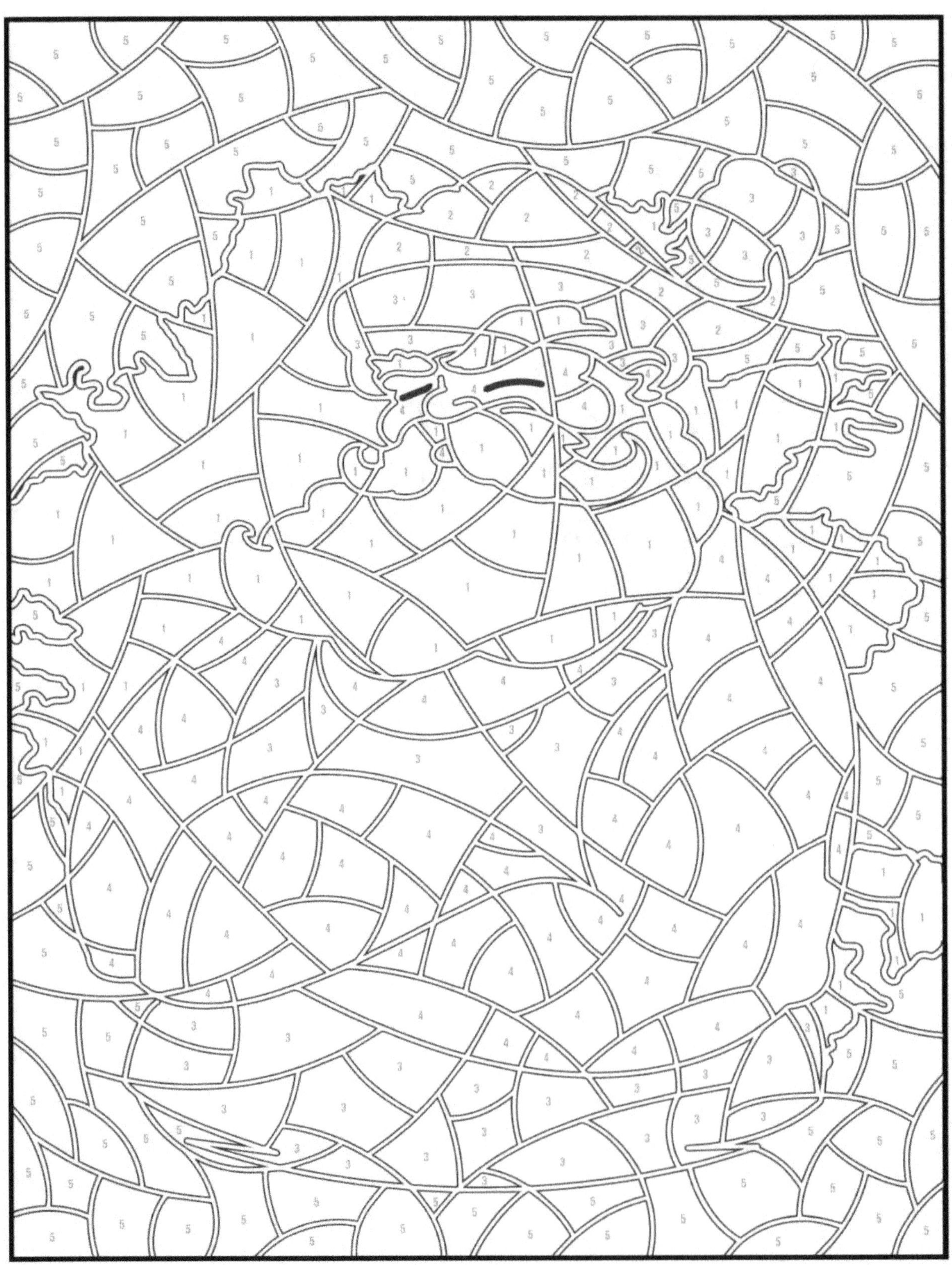

1	DARK GREEN	2	RED
3	WHITE	4	LIGHT BROWN
5	DARK GRAY		

(1)	WHITE		(2)	DARK ORANGE
(3)	YELLOW		(4)	RED
(5)	DARK BROWN		(6)	DARK GREEN
(7)	LIGHT BLUE		(8)	MEDIUM BLUE
(9)	BLACK			

(1)	YELLOW	(2)	RED
(3)	LIGHT GRAY	(4)	LIGHT BROWN
(5)	WHITE	(6)	LIGHT BLUE
(7)	LIGHT PURPLE	(8)	GREEN
(9)	BROWN	(10)	LIGHT GREEN
(11)	ORANGE	(12)	LIGHT PINK

1	LIGTH GRAY		2	PURPLE
3	YELLOW		4	MEDIUM GREEN
5	MEDIUM BROWN		6	LIGHT PINK
7	WHITE		8	LIGHT BLUE
9	RED			

(1)	GREEN		(2)	LIGHT GREEN
(3)	YELLOW		(4)	ORANGE
(5)	RED		(6)	LIGHT BLUE
(7)	VIOLET		(8)	PURPLE
(9)	LIGHT BROWN		(10)	GRAY
(11)	LIGHT GRAY		(12)	MEDIUM BROWN
(13)	LIGHT RED			

1	RED	2	DARK RED
3	GRAY	4	LIGHT BLUE
5	LIGHT BROWN	6	YELLOW
7	BLACK	8	WHITE
9	DARK GREEN		

1	YELLOW	2	DARK GREEN
3	LIGHT PINK	4	LIGHT BLUE
5	RED	6	ORANGE
7	BLUE	8	PINK
9	LIGHT GRAY	10	LIGHT GREEN
11	BLACK		